DETROIT AS BARN

OTHER BOOKS BY CRYSTAL WILLIAMS

Troubled Tongues (Lotus Press, 2009)

Lunatic (Michigan State University Press, 2002)

Kin (Michigan State University Press, 2000)

DETROIT AS BARN

poems by

Crystal Williams

[signed] G H Hill

2·28·14

To My Portland Poetry
Family —
with thanks for
your continued
support and
community
building.
Be well.
Light + Love,

G.H.

LOST HORSE PRESS
Sandpoint, Idaho

Cover Art by James Edward Scherbarth. "Nebraska" (red barn), 16" x 20" oil / cold wax. Other artwork—paintings, photography, digital montage & art jewelry—may be viewed online at www.jamesedwardscherbarth.com.
Author Photo by Owen Carey
Book & Cover Design: Christine Holbert

FIRST EDITION

This and other LOST HORSE PRESS titles may be viewed online at *www.losthorsepress.org*.

LIBRARY OF CONGRESS CATALOGING-IN-PUBLICATION DATA

Williams, Crystal, 1970–
[Poems. Selections]
Detroit as barn : poems / by Crystal Williams.—First Edition.
     pages cm
Includes bibliographical references.
ISBN 978-0-9911465-0-5 (alk. paper)
I. Title.
PS3573.I448414A6 2014
811'.54—dc23
                    2013045889

This book is dedicated to Detroiters
and to my uncle Robert E. Gumbleton
who taught the bitty girl of me to love poetry.

TABLE OF CONTENTS

OMEN

It is Fall in Detroit
& though it is time
for the living world
to take stock,
shed its weak
& protect its strong,
it is odd how the goldfinches
(so many!) are falling
as if muted memories.
Each morning
a new soft body
lay golden & dead
at my door.

Detroit turned out to be heaven, but it also turned out to be hell.

—*Marvin Gaye*

EXTINCTION

> All the new thinking is about loss.
>
> —*Robert Hass*

Like a diseased lung, the city is shutting down
& the parks are first to go.
The grass is long-toothed & wicked,
not grass at all, mostly weeds,
their tough tongues covered with trash.
& the trash is all magic:
it mysteriously appears & disappears.

Beside it today, lovers lie.
& beneath the goldfinch on its branch,
lovers sit on the bench. & another pair,
oddly entwined, roll down the street,
she on his lap, her head on his shoulder,
he sitting straight in an electric blue
motorized wheelchair, a bony arm cradling her back.

Oliver cocks his head because they are odd.
His glistening snout pokes the air
as if to taste what sort of love this is,
this homeless love, this dirty in the grass love,
this broke-down park bench,
middle-of-the-empty-street love,
which is all about holding on to something,
I think, stroking his sweet head,
which is nothing more
than a long, slow song about loss.
This neighborhood. Love. Detroit.
The purple martin overhead. The dog with his cancer.
These paramours amid their abandonment.
Something is always dying.

Brush Park is so much like the city
it is nothing more than the city:

mansions burnt or shackled by time or remade
into monuments to fortitude & foresight.
& amid the ruins, people insistent & loving.

This panorama is what life looks like in my city
where loss & cliché wear the same tight dress,
where music is exquisite & slow
& nothing more than a moan on most days
& then too, on most nights.

But these crazy lovers, in the weeded grass,
high on something, eyes full of magic,
some wispy memory, the life before this life,
the possibility of a perfect & round orange,
make me happy with their surprise
& stubborn headedness.

& as the wind rustles the weeds' spiky fingers,
hikes a bag across the street,
fluffs Oliver's poodle ears,
another sound begins its haunt:
Something lonely,
something approximating
the sound of extinction,
proof of an exact & impending death:
an echo
perhaps, a trill
of the last Heath Hen,
small avian spine gone from the earth
seventy years ago,
his throat coarse & quivering with need.
There were people beneath him that last day too,
listening to his beak bleating & bleating for a mate.

How odd that these lovers in the thickets
almost fool me into believing something more
than the facts, that ambering history,
this bleak branch.

IDIOM

Yesterday   the clouds resembled   my mother's eyes
        gray & varying.   I was prayerful   & slick with sweat
    unconvinced of everything   but the sky.
Something was   just out of reach.   Somewhere
        a language promising   revelation.   Last night
    the mute African woman   with the wide mouth   &
        thin skin   showed me her palms.
They were covered   frantic   with white symbols.
    She held them   so close to my face   my eyes strained.
        I was supposed to read these.   But
        it was a foreign language   & symbols   my undoing:
I tried & I tried   & tried   until   my stomach rolled
    my eyes teared & blurred.   All the while   she smiled
    rubbed my head white   until my hair was gone
& I was   bald   & small   & damp with sweat.   &
        all the while I knew: She is loving me.
We stayed like this   her hands on my head   my body
wet with fever   from trying to know.   We loved
    like this   all of the day.   Silence   all of the day   until
    there was nothing more to do   but sleep on the dirt
amid the birds   cheeping   savannah   at my front
        wooden door of her hut   at my back   blue whale voices
booming   & humming beneath me.   & where she rubbed
    warmth.   When I woke   my whole head   was afire
my whole head   aflame.   Today
        the museum's curator tells us   that white
on the African face means   Spirit   spirit   strong spirit
love spirit   spirit leading   the way.   & I say again:
    fire. I say   again: flame.

3

STRICTURE

after Romare Bearden's *The Conjurer*

Through the *Live, Love, Laugh* shop window
I sometimes watched Stella's gnarl of a body
shamble up the block, hunched-back black stick bruja,
angry white hair & kohled eyes swathed in teal, orange
& white—her smoke trained against gods & devils,
our imperceptible offenses, dragging her bag of skulls &
heather, overhead crows circling & cawing like sorcerers.
Her voice was the first real knowing I had
that among us something is terribly wrong—
her cursing black dog soundtrack, that snarl & howl
eating up everything in Greektown, leaves & lamb
& sweet syrup baklava. For some unspoken reason,
she wasn't shuttled off. & I wondered
the things we wonder about strangeness, the foreign body,
how it was when she bathed or slept or danced,
from whence it came, at sun's ebb to which it went.
It's my fault, really. Had I been tending to matters
Live, Love, Laugh, I would have missed her raging that day,
how it eagerly smacked their laughter dead, the girl
dropping her pastry, father yanking son, their six
legs flung to flee, the small, sane glint & grin of it,
how she turned to examine me—black irises soft &
speaking a new, ugly language, which opened in me something
I will not name. When she nodded & smirked, I nodded back.
In my hand is that, a 20-year old seed, which I roll & roll
& worry, wondering, what was that language & ~~when will~~
how do I stop its brutality blooming in me?

PEOPLE CLOSE TO YOU

after Herbert Woodward Martin & Christine Rhein

I

She asks if she can sit on the bench & it is that kind of day in Santa Monica, slow & gentle so that when she sits, properly, like a teacher or the pudgy mother of a girl named Marilyn, in unison you raise your round faces. The wind hefts the voices of your deadlings. They are serious & sorrowful women, full of warnings, but today seem content to let you be, saying only, *Child, be thankful, open your chest, that great cavern, to our other sister.* & so you watch the sea.

Who knows what the woman beside you hears: there are so many languages in the world & your tongue is tied to this one. So you sip iced tea & lean a bit forward into them, your gone women, your sages, who seem to be stroking your head. You begin to imagine the ocean floor as a cup, the pouty lips of God, the soft foam, the salt as if food, tasting sweet & clear.

II

When she turns to you, you think she might say something about the sea's beauty, about the sun's slow emergence, how salt tastes on the tongue. Instead she says: *I   am   hungry*. Tenderly, as if this is her name, the fact of it blooming in front of you & she smiles. *Sister, I would give you food, but I cannot*, you: holding up your empty hands though you have just eaten. You have a wallet full of food. & she smiles again. & she begins to rise, as if an apparition, moves back into her crevice her body no more than a crevice, an intersection for two opposing points. She nods & lingers a moment before turning her face to the sorrowful voices of your deadlings who moan, Oh.

III

When she emerges from a corner at the drive-through on a Detroit night, her eyes hollow, body stiff & dirty she might screech, her need so black, so dark & dangerous, explain how she too emerges in tatters from a darker crevice no more than a crevice—vile, angry. *Sis*, can you help? *Get back*, you say, fear seeding itself. She smirks, you think. It's hard to tell, the dark takes even that of her triumphs. & again, you: *Don't!* & you mean, emerge from the dark. Your hand grabs the box of chicken. *No*, you say. *Jesus!* & she smiles again. & she begins to retreat, as if an apparition, moves back into her crevice, her body no more than a crevice, an intersection for two opposing points. She nods & lingers a moment before turning her face to the sorrowful voices of your deadlings who moan, oh, oh.

IV

When she turns to you, when she emerges from a corner at the drive-through on a Detroit night, her eyes hollow, body stiff & dirty, you think she might, she might screech, her need so black, say something so dark and dangerous about the sea's beauty, about the sun's slow emergence, explain how she too emerges in tatters from a darker crevice, no more than a crevice, how salt tastes on the tongue, vile, angry. Instead she says: I   am   hungry. Sis, can you help? Tenderly, as if this is her name. *Get back!*, you say, fear seeding itself, the fact of it blooming in front of you. & she smiles. She smirks. You think: It's hard to tell. The dark takes even that of her triumphs. *Sister, I would give you food*, and again, you don't, *but I cannot,* holding up your empty hands. & you mean, emerge from the dark. Though you have just eaten, your hand grabs the box of chicken. You have a wallet. Full of food, *No,* you say, *Jesus! &* she smiles again. & she begins to rise, retreat, as if an apparition, moves back into her crevice, her body no more than a crevice, an intersection for two opposing points. She nods & lingers a moment before turning her face to the sorrowful voices of your deadlings who moan: *Oh, oh, oh.*

POINT OF IMPACT

Begin at the point of impact: the moment your mother leaves your father, not just
as any woman deserts a man, abusing his heart—but when she leaves him to die
in the nursing home, his body old, his heart abandoned, neither half
strong enough to sustain the other—that impact. Begin your
remaking there, not with the details of her cold back
turning, twisting in the wind like a leaf, which
to your father's rheumy eyes must have
appeared easy. Not there, but with the
first note, the dark node on her
heart that over the years grew
& grew until she too died
of it. Begin in that
moment where you
have taken your
lessons, at this
desk, which
is wet &
covered
with the
belief that
at root, people
are not good but
failing, which is not
an admission
so much as a
prayer.

ENLIGHTENMENT

She is merging onto the Edsel Ford Freeway
in a car no longer made,

in a city that no longer makes it,
talking on her cellular phone, slouched to the left,

fingernails purple & red & caging the wheel,
head cocked & foot heavy.

In pursuit of a race car,
she has bought a roll of black duct tape,

has rolled three racing stripes
down the sedan's hood

as if she has been whispering with Buddha
& he said, *Sister, relinquish your resistance,*

your discomfort, forsake your ego.
Which she has done,

which is what it means to want
but not have

in a city stacked with desire,
to know that desire is our most ruinous trait,

the moment in the morning
when you decide to be unsatisfied & unhappy.

Our want is just one of many in a line of wants
& the line of wants is ancillary to the line of needs.

People close to you are hungry
& you have ignored it.

People close to you have lost their jobs.
Today somebody's mother has died.

Today somebody's child has been murdered.
Today some body lost sight.

& your Lumina runs.
Your Lumina runs well; Luminosity,

woman: No one is coming to save you.
There is nothing from which to be saved.

MINDFULNESS

for Sasheen Allen

Bermuda Shorts is at the bus stop in a shock-yellow shirt,
 yellow cap, & matching yellow-&-black sneakers,
  is looking not unlike a person dressed as a bumblebee—& is thirsty.

Across the street is Starbucks, leaving him with options:
  the bus or thirst. But this is Detroit,
   city of bad-attitude-drive-slow-as-you-wanna bus drivers.

The bus will be late. So Bermuda runs through the traffic,
  which isn't traffic as it was but as it is, which is pitiful & slow & so
   no hard hassle, & buzzes into & up to the counter

where he puts on a show: breathes so hard that Apostle Brown
  looks up from his paper & frowns at Bermuda's jive-acting
   bumblebee butt. Bermuda gasps for water & is told,

"We don't *give* water," to which he rejoins
  "I can't get a glass of *water*?!"
   the bugs his eyes bulging. "Can't do it,"

Annoyed Barista says, mouth tight as a fist,
  to which Bermuda puffs, "Why not?!"
   Which was when Manager Barista—

head bald & shiny as a mirror,
  eyes moving across the spine of her memories
   where they rest

on an unexpected indentation,
  a small, persistent curve of kindness—
   says in her vermouthy way, "Well,

12

we typically sell water. But,
   (sighing & shaking her bald head)
      hold on," before moving to the faucet.

That, sir,
   is when you should not
      have gotten brand new & yelled, "Hurry up!"

You'd
   have done better,
      Bermuda,

to quietly watch the small back of her turn
   & be thankful for the moment of her familiarity
      & be thankful for the moment of her

thankfulness. It is good to remember:
   when someone is giving
      a thing they need not give—

a glass of water, a smile, what love they can muster—
   we are wise to feel stroked
      by the warm genius of a world

that does not motor on just reciprocity & sense,
   but on something altogether more
      mysterious & splendid.

WHAT THE MEMORIES SAID

You, woman, bearing your losses,
the dog's leash taut in your hand,
how can you so blind & quickly
pass us on your morning walks?
Haven't you yet learned
there are happenings on planes
you do not see?
The dog knows we are here & have
crucial news. When he stops
& presses his muzzle to the air,
can't you see him sniffing at our feet?

FEEDING DETROIT

All the mouths are rupturing, spreading their
wide red gums, teeth straight as a city block, tongues
flapping like angry fish. Mrs. Elvina Smith hears 'em a ways
off: opining, green—they claim, but for sure blistering &
hot. They wanna turn it all—her gone people, her
house & yard into some sort of citified farm. Evacuate folks

left to what they callin' "blight." Move her among folks
closer to town. Who's gonna be fed, she wants to ask their
dumb mouths, by the so-called plants they gon' grow on her
land? Pft. She'd ask the shiny-shoes & waggling tongues,
but ain't no body here. Nothin's here save her, her house &
the rowdy cemetery of this block. On good weather days, away

from the blue house her & Thomas bought, she waddles way
down memory's trail, drags her hurt hips past the kind folk
& their doings long dead: Mavis' cherry pie, Elvin's second car &
the Tuesday he enlisted, later the flag bearers & their
dull walk, Thomas' silver heirloom watch. Hears them tongues
as she bakes Pastor's favorite fruit cobbler & too on her

way to Wednesday church. Teeth is even clamped to the hem of her
good blue print skirt! She harrumphs, figures: it's their way
of sayin' I'm obsolete. But I am not! Lord, forgive my tongue,
it's swole with pride. I knows the city's a mess, that these folks
don't know what to do. So I opened your book & read right there:
Blessed is the man who does not walk in the counsel of the wicked. &,

at night the long way off of Africa's been yowling my name &
makes me think that writer was right to say knowing buried her
wonder, 'cause I don't wonder no more. I just wants into their
hollering mouths, wants to sit & scrape all that sickness away.

Lord, forgive my ire, but these is dangerous, disbelieving folk.
She sighs. Shifts her eyes down the block. Mrs. Smith's tongue

longs to say, "Y'all's ruptured, children. Your spirits & tongues
ain't right. You shoulda been taught: to memories, a body bends &
says, *Hello, Friends! What's the past getting up to today? Here, folks
is scared, scarred & moving slow. Disbelief got her
heavy hand on things, chasing everything beautiful & mysterious, away.*
To get right with memories you gotta leave your offerings at their

feet." This is Mrs. Elvina Beulah Smith up from Bessemer in '38, her
tongue chattering as she buries her knowing, its folks & their ways,
laying her garden's most precious prayers along the broken curbside there.

MONOLOGUES FROM DETROIT

Judy: Dancer *Kelly: Daughter* *Ancestors: Chorus*

When you see my body
abruptly halt

           & you must begin
           with the body—container

lights marking to
shadow my face

           a containment

the fact of me
bloating

           with complications

chest heaving with
quickenings

           intrusions

I am showing you

           my small knockings
           & doors

the languages
of my house

           depend on the water's
           shore

my father refuses
the language
of his mother
& so refuses to speak
to his mother

           but the body remains
           an affliction

& so
my grandmother
refuses English, so
refuses her son,

the body is
the only fact

you will come to know
my body

its meat
is a half-teller:

When you see me arc
& bend

imagine magic

moving forward

as silence stretching
across a moment

legs scuttling over
the stage's black floor

you can see how
fiercely my father loved

I am showing you
my grandmother

or his tenor's sad songs

& my grandmother's
constant dragging

& how he revered,
that for which he longed

her continent

& how his warm heart
stooped

around our house

arms shaking

vertebrae misshapen

from the weight
of holding the tarnished tray
where he had lain
his heart &

from lugging Xiamen
& its mountains
to our dinner table.

When my hands
gnarl as if fists

        how greedy
        my fingers were
        with taking.

you are watching
my grandmother's
fingers grab again
the narrowing throat
of a sack or—

        This is another magic
        I can tell

the shape of the
cold mountain
where she left what
we might call love.

        how the heart can be
        it's own cold city

& how she dragged it,
dragged & dragged.

        all of its inhabitants
        shuttering against
        this cold

When I thrust my arms
like daggers, like a dagger:

        I can show you

my grandmother's
eyes' furious glow

        how needles retract

what was I to do
but stand aside, watch
their war,

        moving hopelessly slow;

wearing paths
on the floor:

        how we hungered,
        how we lacked

her sack, his feet,
that mountain of
dead language.

Children,

If you ask for facts,
I say

setting the mouth
to a new language
never works.

When others ask,
"& you?   American?"   *just say*

Me: I am Chinese,

I am Black.

I am.

in Detroit &

a Detroiter
the Detroit River
is my shore.

Your body belongs
to what it belongs.

were I not shushed

When you ask for magic
& accept that you may
get lies:

I might tell you this:
once, girls at school
asked me to join

There is always
a murder of girls,
perched overhead

a school yard game,
& Oh!

I'll give you everything
else, the sparks

their raven eyes

I couldn't help but love

How I leapt!
How I danced!

bright as the cars' crackling,
sharp as the sun,

But everyone was so
loud

the Friday night bass
beats,

& my hands were too
small for their

thumping low-riders
on Monroe street, the

red & slippery ball

their hearts slippery
& dark, saying
you are not ours.

they were so strong

It never works,
trying to belong

Look, I wanted to say,
my body is quick.

do you see, girls?

I can get rid of

No need to grab for

my grandmother's sack

that to which you
do not belong

& look,

Stop trying

Detroit is also my shore!
But my tongue stayed
slack & they stared,
rolled their eyes &
took their ball.

stop your attempts

Sometimes when I stand
beneath the stage's hard
light I gleam like

the boys'
shiny chrome &

their black eyes &

rims

ask: who, on your field,
am I supposed to be?

stop striving for

Who other than this
should I have been?
When you watch me
dance

(Stop!)

or I can tell you about
the bright bud of happy
as we learned to be

watch me
fling my bruised body
to the stage's cold floor,

or

(Stop!)

imagine how the lone
body on the school
bus aches

or the ground-down
nub of a city

When you
see me crawl
tender & slow,

you are watching

(Stop!)

no, wait
I want you first to
understand the
impossible clamping

contortions our body's
hearts make.
I am nothing more than

           the devastation of

soundlessness &

           the interpretation of

air
& I think,

                    you must accept

beyond doubt, I am
in fact

           the interruption

                  the alienation of

America. The other

                  being
                  Other—

When you see—

           my heart's city
           & its unbearable ruin.

When you see me cry
I am showing you
the hushed languages
of my house.

                  & that does not
                  mean we
                  are creatures
                  born of lack.)

NOTHING GOLD CAN STAY

We were exploding
yellows,
the day percussive in our mouths,
the small politics
of bodies, hierarchies
on green vinyl seats.
On the bus,
the shy grew shyer,
nobody sat next to Judy
but Ralph.
No one sat next to Ralph.
& everyday we jostled
for places, full meaning,
the yellow
of our lives sparkling
& sheeny & leaning
its great weight into our selves
& our selves saying, *Yes!* & our selves
saying, *Yes, ours! Yes, more! Yes, yes!*
So when some bean-headed boys
threw rocks & cracked
the brilliant glass of our golden
bus, Mr. Mack,
our cooler than Billy Dee,
stopped in a yellow screech,
cranked the door
& took off after their *No!*

We *oooh'd* & *aaaah'd* & craned our necks
until he returned empty handed,
tee shirt wet, legs bulging & hard from work,
a bit of sweet gone from his eyes,
blaze taking its place.
"I'm sorry, y'all,
I guess Mr. Mack's

just an old fool,"
& cranked the door angrily shut.
        We were too young
                to understand that red
                        crank, that flare in his eyes,
                        the way a man's defeat
                is born of sweat,
        the way his muscles ache
& cry after that fight.
So different than what
        we had found:
                The golden door
                        of our worth.
                        Mr. Mack, no.
                You were no fool,
        our Afro'd salvation,
thundering after darkness
        in platform shoes, gilded
                bells of your pants
                        whipping like wings.

OUTSIDER ART
(or, *In Which Artists Descend Upon & Depict "Detroit"*)

half a city
half a chair
half a folk
half a man
half a mother
half a child
half an affair
half a heart
half a cry

(or maybe)

half a photograph of
half a teeter totter

(propped up by bricks against)

half a digitized sky.

THE ARCHITECTURE OF IMAGINATION: ARS POETICA

for Lighthead, from Chicago

When I tell you I lack imagination, you say *no. No.* But
            I know
  how high I can jump & leap, am nearly flat-footed,
 & am fatter than I once was, more solemn too.
           It's okay.
It's not a complaint. This is what I am thinking
    when I realize the man in front of me on the El
has combed-over a snatch of hair ten inches long & two inches wide,
  a hugely long, hugely wide hairy bridge,
      which makes me think about diameters
 & the over top distance between one ear & another,
the cavernous space beneath that gathers all manner of document—
        the duck & her ducklings
  crossing a South Dakota interstate, impact & inevitability,
    how forlorn eight chicks look in a rearview mirror,
the way fog layers & stacks against a forest floor:
   how clarity & density survive each other, or perhaps,
      require each other,
  how smiles simmer or pop & can mean the same thing—
        all of that magic
gathering beneath an exuberant shiny dome.
      I think
about Chicago's Soldier Field that funky mix of very new & very old & of
  Detroit's Tiger Stadium & its dilapidated walls,
     the broke down streets leading to & from it,
the crowds/not crowds,
    the city/not city—
       I can hear wailing
 & it is old & accustomed to being misunderstood—
    the fight on the ground to do with definitions
  & history.
    Some people want to keep it, others to tear it down—
where there is old, significant beauty,

opportunity, we gawk, say

Eh, yeah, it was nice

*but costs so much . . .—*so

unlike Chicago

who bends to lap the feet of its ruins

& then gathers them in big meaty hands,

tends & mends. Re-ups, you could say.

This may be the real difference between the imagination & its lack.

Maybe this is what's wrong with America, I think

as I begin to count the comb-over's strands.

It's a ridiculous pursuit

& I should find another place to sit.

He is dangerous & his brown suit is layered in fine dust & gravel,

as if a portent. This is metaphoric, you know.

Dust is not what his suit holds. It holds a tribe of tiny brown men

all thinking the same thought: *Woman, you are not that fat*

or that sober. Yours is a different work.

But by then I am too deeply obsessing about him, his comb-over,

your lightheaded way of walking in the world,

kicked up in the air

like some giant animated soldier

doing something akin to Nutcracker kicks,

knees & feet straight & strong as plutonium arrows.

Also, I am thinking of the imagination on a cold island,

shivering & alone, starving,

but beneath an orange sky, wanting nothing more

than a pen

to document the facts:

Each morning this man

lays that bizarre grouping

of ten-inch hairs proudly across his balding dome,

persuading them by some magic

I don't care to know. Maybe he is giving us all directions:

reach, however unlikely, for the unreachable. An

American Hero lyric.

An installation,

a performance artist.

But in the world of my world,
           some flat-footed thing has to happen when,
       like everyone, like everything,
the strands give way to gravity.
    & even though he intends to offer some artistic & magnanimous
invitation or suggestion,
                  there is the quiet moment when,
                       sans sad acrobatics, the acrobat—
    just out of the shower, strands loosed & soaking—
stands across from a hazy reflection
of what is wrong with America:
                       his fingers reaching for gel.

DETROIT AS CHIHUAHUA

from Chicago, Illinois

Oscar is a serious dog,
a Weimaraner with opinions—serious
& gray is what he is. Big, well-favored.
So when that blinged-out yap of thing,
lead by a piece of yarn (no lie!)
attached to a girl in pencil jeans & a furry vest
stopped at the light,
Oscar did turn & acknowledge them,
but with incredulity
of the sort that settles on people
who bug-eye when you answer their
"Where are you from?" with
"Detroit."
Oscar sniffed that yap of thing
as if to say, "Really?" as if to say,
"But how can this be?"
& then as if shrugging, turned away.
It's like that, being from Detroit.
The Chihuahua—bred mighty & loyal,
its heart & courage bigger than its due—
attached to an absurd tether,
having to chin up against the wind
& all of the shit—debris, cigarette butts,
paper cups—people throw off.
& you've got no say
other than to stand your small, proud ground,
in the stupid dotted sweater
some neurotic misanthrope
has dressed you in. & then
it's having some solipsistic beast
sniff & sniff & turn slowly away,
but not before he lifts his dumb leg

& pees on your head
because he can
& supposes it'll say something
about power & one's place
in the pack.

DETROIT AS THE NIGHT CAGE

The old male's long limbs are peppered
gray, his eyes watch a female fling a baby
onto her back & then their bodies up & up.

She settles well away from him, goes safe & high,
watches him watching, watches the other
females watching, coos her baby & wipes its face.

The old male scratches his ear, swats a fly,
glances behind him where two young males stalk
like hungry boys, hoodlums on the block.

He does this many times, look back & swat, look
sideways & swat. This reminds me of an apprentice
who glibly said to my friend, "I want what you have,"

as if desire is an innocent who need not be fattened
& fed, as if envy is not an action, but a fact.
When he recounted this, my friend's eyes were plaintive,

as if the apprentice's mouth were a dark gorge
into which he had peered & seen his body lain.
That night the young males castrate the old male,

rip him red & wide. Video shows them
working in unison while from another cage
the females screamed dissatisfaction & threw sticks.

We are ahistorical creatures. This is how things come
to pass. The females, kept separate by zookeepers
in order to prevent violence, inspire but cannot thwart

violence, making a new architecture, a new history,
a series of asymmetries scraping each other
until something is dying or dead. & this reminds me of

the old man hobbling across the street, a young man
in a low rider, thumping at the light, pressing
forward, hop, pop, thumping at the light,

& how the old man disapprovingly eyed the young man,
& found behind the glass' glare the quick, raw nature
of what it means to be dying

as seen through the miserly eyes of youth: nothing.
No one's giving commendations for a long, well-lived life.
Dying means nothing more than you are an obstruction,

hobbling against the light. The old man stopped, oblivious
to the green, staring into the blue thump's reflection,
the young man, disgusted, sneered & looked away,

their bodies as if the city, the country—a knowing,
an imprudent shunning—the same body in converging
states of dying. As it was, the keepers found a bloody mess,

the females berating the young males, hollering
& clutching babies close, snubbing the murderers
who sat quietly waiting & swatting. Swatting.

& watching, content with their deed.
When the females stopped grunting,
the young males moved slowly about the cage,

taking everything in, the females,
their babies, the keepers on high alert,
the constraints of their new city,

& then the other,
the other, surveilling
& thumping flies.

CANCER RISING

Rochester Hills, Michigan

In the skin
      cancer center's
            waiting room
the old men
      have formed a clan of chinos
            & baseball caps. Their stomachs
pout & lips dry. They are varying,
      in stages of being healed &,
            from what I gather,
convinced their world is ending:
      Different animals are well-side,
            drinking good &
deeply. They suspect
      the world has finally turned
            its cold fist on them.
They eye me.
      Their youngest leers, occasionally
            waves his nasty hand,
licks his chops. But I am no sweet meat.
      I leer back:
            In my city,
We are thirsty,
      thin-eyed & rangy.
            Our healthy make deep ruts
to the suburbs
      to raise young. Now their young
            are in *our* domain,
sniffing along curb edge
      beneath my window, on bikes,
            appraising, searching
for a new place to exist.
      & I too am a low growl
            & froth. The men's voices

rise, foam, hiss about their water,
land. Eyes darken, shift
from each other & back.
This how battles begin, as churnings
in the fearful, grievous bellies
of fattened women & men.
I lower my eyes,
decide
today to search & pray
for the hidden sack
in which we each stash:
a full moon,
a God, the gods, tatters
of kindness, four halved plums.
Without it
we are left quivering,
stock piling
for torpor's cold,
when all the body understands
& uses for sustenance is encased—
iced over or dead—
when it is malnourished & slow,
& all you can depend on
is your own disbelief
in nature's grace, your sly hoarding
eyes—in the waiting room,
at the window—
your stupid animal,
starved
& hungry for blood.

THE WAY HOME

the water is not wet   but soft   & the whale's name is Kyra,

     she says.   Like the old African woman   with the symboled hands,

she   too   has been waiting for me.   In my dream   her voice

sounds like   a well of magic   a deep cone echoing my name.

Her back   is soft as water   & I am supposed to climb

     onto its long path   for the journey   is great

& the ride   uneasy.   She tells me   we are going home

     & home is many tongues away   beneath

another beneath   which rests between the reefs   of hunger

     & hungering.   She means: the water there

     is so hot   the body feels nothing   but its heart's breath.

     By now   I am smarter, know not to ask   how we get there:

No map,   just magic calling & calling   echolocation making our path.

     Her eyes are blue   blue blue   gems.   The ocean,

I know,   is her heart's water-making.

Those great blue promises   blink & blink   as I slide on her back

     trying to make sense of her enchantment: Do not ask others

for answers your heart knows.   This too is like a grain   bulgar, rice

     I fold into my hand.   Later I will feast & feast,

feast myself fat.   The ocean's other creatures   wink as we pass

babies gleam &   flip their newness.   & this means, "Be well, sister."

Their families   remind me   seem something   I may have once

had   & I stare   but the water grows   too dark

& Kyra warns me   *hold tight*   *we are moving into a different beneath*

     the way home   burbling   in the throat   of this magic vehicle

this enchanted animal   who seems so strong   & all mine.

DETROIT AS BREWSTER PROJECTS

It must be like this in Iraq,
after a bombing,
the killing. So many
tall, windowless buildings,
mattresses propped
against openings, silence
making the thing
more barbarous.
Danger & death
bloom, balance
in the wind
as if pregnant
heads of weeds.
Always the same
amputee rolling
down the street,
swathed in dark,
fuming garments,
something brutal
about his eyes,
his arms powerful
& veering across the line
set on the street
towards your car
causing you to shift,
swerve. & some other
vacant body standing
on the sidewalk, staring
into the oblong sky.
Another's back turns a corner:
Something is happening
out of sight, some life
beneath this life,
in this, these
discarded buildings,

some drug
perching its swart self
against the brink
of light. You can feel
life brimming,
its blistering hand
twisting, its shadowy heart
making a home
in the small, daily changes
of the place: a mattress
two feet to the right,
the tattered cloth hanging
from a third floor window
when yesterday
it was four floors up.
People perch here,
their bodies a line
you dare not cross.
You do not heed
the STOP sign
waving its angry head.
You speed up when possible
drive around the entire thing,
the compound
& its recreation center,
the fifteen buildings,
the almost-town houses, parks,
the tennis-turned-basketball
courts, ceded playgrounds,
grass & trees not dead
but not as they are meant to be,
bits of fire & char
edging everything, people,
addicts wandering
their slow way along,
weaving in & out
of the torn & near-gone

chicken fencing as if
their bodies & minds
are fight partners,
legs & backs shuffle & slide,
their red eyes like mortar,
like shells.   The city
means to tear it down,
this & what it means.
But today, some man,
the fool, has brought
a clutch of children
to this desert. They are
swinging on the rotted wood
plank of the teeter totter.
Their mangy Rottweiler
unsteady & tied to a tree.
He watches as the children,
bundled against the cold,
learn to balance & shriek.

SIGHTINGS

The path from this village to that is untranslated.

—*Robert Haas*

The blond girl sitting next to me with severe hair
& too many bangs is named Jemima.

Her voice is musical, light, but privileged, already growing aloof.
We are in first class, her mother & brother a row behind us,

leaving one state of being, entering another.
They reside in London but are schooled in Paris,

move between the two each week.
We are two rows of changelings.

I am from Detroit, know the body's divide,
am a dry mouth twirling its troubled, scrapping tongue,

my mind's muscular hinge translating frantically
between England & France, Detroit & Madrid, white,

black—this village & that. Today, beyond the fact
of this swivel mouth mind,

we have little of consequence in common,
Jemima & I, bodies casting as one through the air.

We sit silent, though
when I say hers is a name I know,

"Thank you. It *is* popular," she pips. "Yes," I yield. Take care,
pilot, there is blue so close below. Blue

brilliance & warmth.

40

An ocean—cosmos beside me & beneath me,
    a life beneath this life—
    a watery world of meaning not mine

    & never meant for me.
    & here is an unlikely first: I smile at Jemima. O nemesis,

    O nag, O shark & minnow, O
    voice grown small & small.

THE LIFE BENEATH THIS LIFE

I

Evening is becoming at the coffee shop
& everything seems mixed, layered,
bodies ripple with transition's promise.
Hours ago our group was all splash & banter:
Last week, a woman shot a boy who snatched her purse.
But there is, "too much violence & loss," I protest.
Johnny Dawson chimes: *He was taking* something.
It doesn't matter what. If she hadn'ta clipped him,
he woulda done it again & he mighta done it to you.
Johnny thinks I'm rich, that wealth breeds optimism,
naiveté: *I wanna be like you, walking your poodle,*
drinking coffee, sitting here all day
staring out the window. You got it good!
"I am not rich, Johnny. I'm a poet.
I'm working when I am watching."
Right, he says, & his voice holds a note
which would be the strong rich song
of a sad, hard field south of here,
were he let it go, which would make me
a pale woman at the window
were he to let it go. But he does not let it go.
He holds it tight. *Rich*, he murmurs.

II

Here, we are an ecosystem,
each gone back in our respective bays:
Johnny Dawson to his corner & muted porn,
Numbers Runner to his adoring, playful court.
Apostle Brown, Brian & Keith, have gone,
are somewhere in their homes' hum.
A sea change: the night patrons are on us—
heavier with their slow chaos & tide.
I take this newness as difference,
cold water tightening my limbs,
feel myself a reef, a harbor
into & out of which life flows.
Then Rashad enters, is gentle
across from me, his mouth soft, fleshy.

He is a teacher & collects stories,
bears them in the conscious way he walks:
A girl whose mother came to the school
so high her body took the shape of a comma
on the Principal's office chair.
A girl who cussed him, mouth
red & crusted as a battlefield.
Their bodies trapped as eddies, all them.
Minnows among sharks.

In Rashad's eyes, past flecks of amber,
Buddha sits watching,
Allah's weary hand moves over his beard.
This quiet stroking makes easy
thoughts of sex, or perhaps, loving,
being filled—& the cold cone of absence,
how often what is lacking
finds space in our body, whispers its suggestion,
perhaps demands a shape.

III

We watch the night shift workers outside tar
potholes for the Orchestra patrons.
The way from their suburb
to this intersection is rough. Tamp. Tar.
Tamp. It's a system, proof. Every year
they tamp & tar. & again tamp & tar. & again
every year. My friend insists
she does not understand how this reflects
racism & oppression, does not understand
how racism & oppression work,
says I am wrong to say we all fear
& so we all estrange, we all fear
& so we all hate, we are born of fear
& so difference—tamp, tamp, tar—
is what we uphold & make. We argue until
what drifts between us is hot spit,
spume. She is smart so I know she is lying.
She is only a mother, cradling
something sweet & blond in her arms,
on a beach, turning to deflect the sun's bright
glare, or more likely, turning like a priest
towards an altar she'd prefer. Either way,
they are off the hook, Rashad says. His
fourteen year-olds are tethered, two
nineteen year-olds are illiterate,
"Illiterate?!" I squall.
Maybe words here & there, but yeah,
he says, functioning & illiterate.

What more is there to say
when the difference is a horizon?
We watch the men tamp, tamp,
tar, smooth the years' neglect.   "Why
did your student cuss you out?" I ask.

44

It's just like that, he shrugs, all of them are
like that, mouths as gardens of destruction,
explosions where death is seeded & blooms.
Lost, he says. I nod, looking around, "Or,
drowning. Everyone strong enough
has pushed away."

IV

Lake Jocassee, "Place of the Lost One,"
is another man–made catastrophe
where curious people dive to recover
remains of a town, a lodge, old Cherokee
pathways transcribing the way
from one village to another, a language
made of the valley settling between its mountains,
a graveyard, the frigid water of four lakes,
the valley's Oconee Bell blooming. Gone.
Water-logged. A language is a comparative system.
& that is all it is: The tall tree
on the valley's eastern edge
is only tall if the valley exists.
"I love you" only means
if there is a *you* after *I*.
Former residents have no way to describe
where the family bones lay. They cannot
say, *past the lodge & through town on the*
yellowing knoll. She's waiting for you
close to the field of blooming Bells.
This is how a heart's language is lost.
It is made to use unfamiliar codes.
Rashad's student & her heart's language
are pinned beneath our country's
turbulent, wet morose. This is how we make,
you & I: we stack. A life beneath a life.
A body atop a body. Notion atop fact.

V

"How do you face them everyday?"
Watching me, he sighs, They're ours.
She's trailed her momma since thirteen
in hot pants on the stroll, men gouging
& digging into her light. Rashad says,
preparing to leave, Of course she cussed me out.
When her mouth is not full of some man,
it is a black smoker, fuming red.

That's fucked up!, laughs Johnny Dawson.
Surprises you, don't it? I nod, confused by his glee.
Because you're not part of this, he sings,
clicking his fingers, waving his callused hand, *us,*
pointing over my shoulder through the window
to the corner where an old man wobbles at the light.
I torque & turn, see—my reflection
through the window, my body
like my friend's, turning, turning
from what Johnny is saying.
But truth is not a solitary endeavor.
So I turn back, express to him another:

"Johnny Dawson, you do not know what I am,"
the dark sky deepening as I rise.
Once, a flurry of leaves in Alabama told me
I too have another name. Mine is an adopted body—
of no womb I can name, begun
at the moment of birth,
beginning, each moment a birth.

"I am a daughter of these streets.
Somewhere in this city
are an entire people belonging to me,"
I say, stumbling, packing my bag.
"I might even be related to you.

A whole life, Johnny,
beneath this grit-to-gloss life.
But for luck, that girl in her hot pants
could be me." You're talking to two people,
Johnny, the woman before you & the woman
before the woman before you.
He pauses, frowns & then again
tightens his note, *Naw,*
the problem with you
is you want *to believe we're beautiful.*
But, he frowns, *you're wrong & you should stop*
reaching for what ain't reaching for you.

NORTHERNER

Bessemer, Alabama, 2010

On the way to my father's hometown
where myth has been calling my name,
kudzu has been set upon the tall, sad trees,
their limbs & wise, old mouths.
It snakes green along the highway
as if a fellow traveler,
binds one tree's limbs to another's.
I stop roadside, watch the impregnable wall,
listen to the ravenous stranger
weave a story about endings. The kudzu
devours every bit of empty space
between limbs & leaves,
as if it is history,
leaves only the refuge of its consumption,
resplendent filler: vines & fronds—
fancy words on the sky's blue
page, coiled & choking
what once might have sprouted
from my father's dead mouth:
What's left is only rumored
limbs, rumors of individuals'
gnarled brown hands, branches
gagged beneath an aggressor's,
waving warnings. We are all bound,
Babygirl. That is all. That is all.

THE EMBRACE

I have never been
& likely will never go
to the spot on the earth
where my mother's ashes are buried.
People do not understand.
Their eyes harden.
But I take comfort in the facts:
the grass there lengthens,
rusted leaves fall & rot,
industry's soldiers
march across the letters of her name,
& today, when the small girl in the book shop
in her white toile princess dress twirls & twirls,
her throat warbling with glee,
jumps into the laughing eyes of her mother,
their arms & bodies clasped,
their heat radiant & necessary
as if they had never been torn apart,
my mother's papery arm
is again entwined with mine
as we plod from the hospital ward's shower stall
down a dim hall, thin cotton gown
tight across her behind, when she,
in one of her last miracles—
as if a lithe Fred Astaire
& against all evidence—
kicks both feet in the air heel-to-heel
& squeals, "I am clean! I am clean!
Oooooh-weeeee! I am clean!"
Thus her eyes & bliss. Thus her arms
& bliss. There she is. My mother.
In that embrace. There.

AT THE WATER

for A. Van Jordan, from Detroit's RiverWalk

Fifty feet in front of their mother
they lurch towards the dog sitting at your feet,
an eruption of "Yeses!", hands & arms
like new branches twisting skyward.

Their mother calls, "Don't touch that dog!"
& because they are good kids, smart, they heed & halt
three feet from me as she makes her slow way towards us.

All morning I've watched some version of this birthing:
what parents give & cost their children.
But history is nothing more

than a chronic transfer of limitations,
a way of understanding
who we might have been.   & who we are

is bodies born of shackles, water.
What these children do in the moment of desire
when the world offers beauty

is an anchor, a shackle forcing them
to yield & gawk at the dark tongue of "no,"
at the foot of a tenacious history circling the edges,

snapping its warnings, making their mother leery
of even a dying, toothless poodle. & so
it's always the white children who claim the dog's body,

their branchy limbs & excited eyes
free of history's shadow.
& Oliver is all possibility:

patient & giving. Here, in the soft fur, in the *Yes*
is where so much, perhaps everything
is lost.

But then there are two brown children still standing
three feet shy of me, bodies tremorous, humming.
Their mother, her eyes the world's closed doors,

moves past like a storm warning, snips:
"No, I said!
'Come on!'"

The girl is older, already her hands have rubbed
history's back, her body turns towards the storm.
But the boy's eyes move slowly,

take in every bit of the dog's beautiful mountain, as if
because he understands something about his mother & sister
& self, he must savor, as if he *will* relent to the fact of

his David
& their Goliath—
but he will not bow.

His sister grabs his hand.
Their mother is getting too far away.
Maybe she is seven. He four. Static

for her pull & his tug. But outside of history's reach,
he rallies, moves closer.
"His name is Oliver," I say.

The boy considers me then looks down the River Walk,
says quietly to his mother's dark, moving back:
"I want to say 'Hi' to Oliver."

& I am broken with imaginings:
the many corner stops, ways of knowing, cops,
the times this black boy will be forced to call out

his innocence's intention to the world.
&, oh, Lord do I want him to be making himself before me,
place-marking this moment,

deciding against the murky back of history—
the keen-tongued mother, the soft pull sister—
who he will become. *It can be done,* I think,

but say, "Oliver knows you do, Baby,
& on another day you two will be *great* friends."
He considers me again, nods & then leaves me with

those wide, black orbs, the young, quiet hands, how he grew
small & small, sprinting towards the dark back of history,
calling, "Here I come, here I come!"

HARBINGER

At the moment the dog dies,
some last good leaves your body,
harbinger, O, you woman
without mother, father, lover,
this dog with his final sweet breath snout.
Omen, O you, lay thee down
in the bracken & brush.
In a morning beyond tomorrow
morning, by some strength not fully your own,
drag yourself to the dirt & wait.
The birds will come with their hopping.
The ants too. In the cold hours
pray they again begin their small work,
their dead dragging.
    For those who want to know,
this is what I say:
there is no competent language for loss.
there is only how we sustain it. & grief,
alas, is no destination. For some of us
she is a cruel spitish companion,
who gnaws on our vertebrae, feasts again,
again, occupies her time—
when she is not waving her symboled hands,
when she is not shrieking her crimson language—
in the muck of our bile & blood.
    When you see us hobbling towards you
understand we should not be standing.
Our spines are abnormal, preternatural,
reconstituted by a darkling
you do not care to know.
Brother, Sister, I beg you,
honor this thing with whom I walk,
who clamps my hand.
If ever you see me smiling,
call it a miracle
& turn your face to God.

IN THE BLACK BOX THEATER

for Marilyn McCormick
& the performing arts students of Cass Technical High School

This is an argument for happiness—
everyone is slightly musty as bodies are
when we are most ourselves,
the children sprawl across
the laps of their friends
the girls' hair springing out of their ponytails
like paltry lances, the boys
wiping spittle from their mouths,
the girl with the wet-n-wavy weave
wrenching the thing back into place.

They are rehearsing the musical *Rent,*
bodies dank from running the stage
& making it all seem beautiful,
the way art is supposed to look, easy,
so that people watching can imagine
something beyond the turmoil of production,
how feet blister or throats bleed or
how hungry the actors are.
This is what they are doing:
learning to give. Their voices
are exhausted, shake from singing
about devastation so that now
when they talk you can especially hear
their unfiltered child. & they are so young,
but know things, discuss the difference
between rebellion & revolution.
Their teacher presses,
sends them digging
in the bulkhead of their lives. Hands go up.
Someone mentions an East Side food line riot.
Another says softly: chaos & sadness
are cousins to revolution.

You could leave it like this, from your vantage point:
the teacher, her back, the red chair,
sloppy bodies, & this black box:
the floors black, the walls & ceiling
& children black, the curtains, everything
black but the small light hitting them here
& here, resting on the chicken leg of a boy,
on the African butt of a girl, but undirected,
not yet fully set for the stage
leaving this to happen in a dim haze
that warns of the uninspired life.
You could say this box might be the city
& stop at how dark & black & bleak. People do.
But then, there are the children
learning their value, how to make it so
& how to hear & hold & when the script
deems it necessary, turn their tongues clear
of the city & its slow drawl, Alabama & its long arm,
how to turn the tongue to cut,
to imagine the world through the flashing
& glossed eyes of art holding her arms open
& saying, *Come, Children, freedom.* This is the children
bursting, reaching & running towards her.

When at a dinner in Massachusetts
a friend leaned his kind face in & asked
about the heart of the city, where it is because,
he said, *In the news it's like Detroit has no heart,*
you understood him to be asking about hope,
& did not fully answer. You hummed,
the deep throat of you urging itself forward & up
to the tender lip of this black box moment,
to the girl of you twenty-five years ago,
how in four years your arms, like theirs, grew strong
& tired, how your eyes learned to see in the dark,
the almost invisible, the possible,
but when he asked, hum was all you could do

because you had forgotten
—the world is so busy & loud
& you have had much goodness—
& this hadn't yet happened.
You back in the city. The city as the country.
Everyone so hungry, so quiet & quaking.
Your intimate knowing of loss & her dark leer.
& also, it hadn't yet happened quite like this:
this picture. The woman, like a mother,
cane on the floor, her leg aching,
stomach booming from the long work
of tending their small & growing miracles,
the damp unlit quality of it all,
her mouth worn & saying: *Yes, Children! Yes!*
the way her fists pump in the air
at each exclamation point,
the tiny points of her thumbs like lights, their eyes,
all of them, awed, & you suddenly
being unable to tell who is sitting
at the foot of whom.

MODELING: DETROIT AS MOTHER

at Cass Technical High School

This is your teacher:
the daughter praying over her mother
the fifty & eighty years of them
standing outside of the black box theater
wavering like lilies.
She is going to smooth her mother's hair.
You watch the hand slow
as it reaches the point
on her mother's face
where the forehead ends
& the gray begins.
Really, nothing is out of place.
But she has made a decision
against today's hard saddenings
so now her fingers
are called to dance & praise
across her mother's hair.
This is the daughter saying
thank you, God.
This is the daughter saying,
thank you, Jesus. This is your teacher
whispering, *Holy. Holy,*
in this corridor in which I walk,
in your theatre where I study. Thank you
for this woman, for how she bends
to kiss her mother's cheek, & for how
like a whisper, the mother,
the mother leans softly forward.

DETROIT AS BARN

for Phil Levine

Gone the hay. Gone the tools. Gone the morning work.
Over there a tractor rusts. Gone the cows, goats,
the slack-tongued mule. Left are owls & rats, fat, wily cats,
& the field where wild weeds grow.

The farmer, they whisper, driving past, knows everything
a body needs to know about dying. You can tell
by how he doesn't bother to paint or prop
the barn's worn wood.

Still, folks click their teeth & wonder on which day,
at what time, the pitiful barn will give. The farmer too
scratches his mighty, balding head.

But he's forgotten the good wood he used,
the hard nails, the family, the friends & their strong backs,
that long ago barn raising, that cider & fine punch.

HOMECOMING

                                                    & when
by some fluke you return, dragging your blue black behind you,
nothing is as it was. The city is stasis,
not dance. Bereavement, not dance. The music has darkened
& stopped its sway, the boulevards are empty theatre.
& who should love this? Who recognizes this? Broken curbs
& potholes & shoes hanging from power lines
& snatches of weave hair blowing like sagebrush. Statues
& statuses. Someone once said that crows are old, wise folks
& today they follow you again, hopping wire to wire, squawk
& squawk until you look up, call: Hey, hey, girl, ain't no other
place knows you, loves you like this, knows that when you shine
out in the big wide, this here is what's sparking your shimmer,
this is the pop, pop, pop lighting your eyes, filling your mouth with stars.
& you nod because the bones of you know
& there was really no escaping
this dance city, this holy morning empty street city,
this dialysis clinic on every other corner city, this be a smart girl city,
this play the harp on Tuesdays & Thursdays city,
this girl-you-look-good-&-we're-called-to-praise-&-lift-you-up city,
this ice-skate city/jazz-dance city, this tote as many talents
    as you can carry city,
this be-whatever-you-want city, this daddy's sweet pea city,
this drive like you want because we're free city, this quiet & quake city,
this we used to build Lumina/Caddy/Explorer city,
this family reunion on Belle Isle/BBQ hot/thump music city,
this momma dressed as a scarecrow on Halloween city,
this Little Alabama City city, this Smokey/Aretha/Florence city,
this FaygoRedPop/VernorsGingerAle city,
this long memory city, this big wheel chipped tooth city,
this johnjohn & veevee & fernando/robyn/karriem city,
this how could you have stayed away for so long city. This
This city, this downbeat to the secret, irrational life of your heart.

NOTES

"People Close To You"

The poetic form, the Contrapuntal (related to the musical term, "counterpoint" which suggests the juxtaposing of two dissimilar harmonies/elements), is loosely employed in the poem's fourth section. While many poets since its invention have used the form, I first heard a contrapuntal read by poet Christine Rhein at a poetry reading in Detroit.

"Feeding Detroit"

At its most robust, Detroit's population topped 1.5 million residents. Current estimates suggest that between 500 to 700,000 people reside in the city, leaving many homes uninhabited and big swaths of land unused. In the late 2000s, a growing conversation (which originated in the 70s) about urban farming and the "greening of Detroit" began to reemerge in response to the many uninhabited and unused blocks in city. The poem paraphrases Chinua Achebe, noted as the African writer.

"Brewster Projects"

When open, the Brewster Projects, also known as the Brewster-Douglass Housing Projects (named after Fredrick Douglass), was the largest public housing development in the city of Detroit.

"Nothing Gold Can Stay"

This title is also the title of a poem written by Robert Frost.

ACKNOWLEDGMENTS

This manuscript's creation was generously encouraged and supported by the MacDowell Arts Colony, Reed College, and a visiting appointment to DePauw University as the Mary Rogers Field Distinguished University Professor of Creative Writing.

I extend my sincere gratitude to Martha Collins, Marilyn McCormack, Carol Moldaw, and Lisa Steinman for their careful attention to this in-process manuscript. Amanda Moore and Yona Harvey listened to and/or read many of these poems and, as true friends do, asked more of me at every turn. David Axelrod was instrumental in ushering this book into the world and I want to thank him again and publicly for his generosity and advocacy. Curtis Bauer and Ross Gay of *Q Avenue Press* served as cheerleaders when I most needed them. I adore you all.

Additionally, I appreciate the enthusiasm of the editors who have published the following poems:

2 Bridges Review: "Northerner," "Nothing Gold Can Stay," "Omen." "What the Memories Said"

Academy of American Poets Poem-A-Day Project: from "People Close to You"

American Poetry Review: "The Architecture of Imagination," "The Embrace," "Modeling," "Sightings"

Connotation Press: "Brewster Projects," "Enlightenment," "Extinction"

PEN America: "At the Water," "In the Black Box Theatre," "The Life Beneath This Life"

Tin House: "Cancer Rising," "Point of Impact,"

The Northwest Review: "Detroit as the Night Cage," "Idiom," "Omen"

The Sun: "Detroit as Barn"

Ploughshares: "Harbinger"

Finally, "Enlightenment" and "Extinction" appear in *Angles of Ascent: The Norton Anthology of African-American Poetry.* Thank you, Charles Rowell and Vivee Francis.